Think Good Thoughts, Do Good Things

Best Nicholaus

Enjoy!

Think Good Thoughts, Do Good Things

Inspiring Quotations and Suggestions for Life

Bret Nicholaus and Paul Lowrie

Authors of the national bestseller *The Conversation Piece*

Warm Words Press
a division of William Randall Publishing

Warm Words Press
a division of William Randall Publishing
P.O. Box 340, Yankton, SD 57078

Cover, graphic, and text design by Ann Lundstrom
(www.demo-graphics-design.com)

ATTENTION: SCHOOLS AND BUSINESSES
William Randall books are available at quantity discounts with bulk
purchase for educational, business, or promotional use.
For more information, contact:
William Randall Publishing, Special Sales Department,
P.O. Box 340, Yankton, South Dakota 57078.

ISBN #0-9755801-3-2

Printed in the United States of America

First Edition: July 2004

10 9 8 7 6 5 4 3 2 1

Think Good Thoughts,
Do Good Things

Welcome!

Over the course of the last ten years or so, we have had occasion to write numerous introductions for our various books. Traditionally they have run three or four pages, explaining to the reader in detail exactly how to best enjoy the book that is in their hands. By contrast, no lengthy introduction is needed for the book you are currently holding. The goal of these pages is simple and straightforward: to help you think good thoughts and do good things! The book will help you do that by providing you with extremely inspiring and thought-provoking quotations and suggestions.

A quick look at the evening news or morning paper makes it more than obvious that what this world needs—and what each of our lives needs—is a lot more good and a lot less negative. Indeed, every one of us must do our part to bring about more good, and we believe that this book can help all of us do that. As the proverbial journey of a thousand miles begins with a single step, so the trip toward a happier and more satisfying life can, in fact, begin with a single quote—or suggestion. You just never know where one of these pages will lead you!

There is, by design, no particular order to the quotations or suggestions; you can open to any page at any time and be inspired by what you find there. You'll see quotes about talent next to quotes about character; you'll find quotes about money next to quotes about prayer. You'll find suggestions on how to help others and suggestions about how to help yourself. In short, all the quotations fall under one general heading: Good thoughts to ponder. Likewise, all the suggestions fall under one general heading: Good things to do.

In a nutshell, that's the book. There is really nothing more that needs to be said concerning it, except this: It is our sincere hope that these pages will truly inspire you to think more positively at all times and do those things which can make the world a better place. Above all else, may the words of this book refresh your soul for all the days still ahead of you.

Enjoy!

Bret Nicholaus and Paul Lowrie

Special Note

In order to bring you *Think Good Thoughts, Do Good Things*, the authors read through more than 10,000 quotations from countless sources; the quotes that are listed in this book represent, in the authors' views, the best of the best. They also wrote hundreds of suggestions of their own before narrowing those down to what they thought were the most important ones; those select suggestions are also contained in this book, interspersed among the quotations.

*W*atch your thoughts;
they become words. Watch
your words; they become actions.
Watch your actions; they become
habits. Watch your habits;
they become your character.
Watch your character; it
becomes your destiny.

FRANK OUTLAW

*S*andwich every bit of criticism between two layers of praise.

MARY KAY ASH

*I*f you take care of the moments, the years will take care of themselves.

MARIA EDGEWORTH

*W*rite a one-sentence mission statement for your life and carry it around with you in your wallet. Remind yourself of this mission statement every day and do all that you can—in every way—to fulfill it. Remember: A mission statement for life is much more than a mission statement about a career; your work can be one means of helping you fulfill your mission, but it must never, ever be the mission itself. Also keep in mind that a great mission statement for life benefits other people, not just yourself.

The true measure of a life is not its duration, but its donation.

CORRIE TEN BOOM

Always bear in mind that your own resolution to succeed is more important than any other factor.

ABRAHAM LINCOLN

*P*eople are like
stained-glass windows.
They sparkle and shine when
the sun is out; but when the
darkness sets in, their true
beauty is revealed only
if there is a light
from within.

ELISABETH KUBLER-ROSS

$\mathcal{L}$earn to let others "have the stage." In your conversations, be very careful not to one-up someone else's stories or statements. (If someone tells you about their wonderful five-day trip to Florida, don't immediately follow it with the story of your glorious ten-day cruise in the Caribbean!) When you try to top what someone else has said, you are implying that what you have to say is far more important than what they have just told you. Always strive to put the interests of others in front of your own.

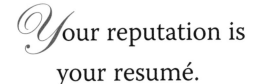

Your reputation is
your resumé.

MADELEINE ALBRIGHT

You're not truly free until
you've been made captive by
some supreme belief.

MARIANNE MOORE

I have always wanted to be somebody, but I can see now that I should have been more specific.

LILY TOMLIN

*A*s you climb your own ladder of success, consciously reach your hand down to bring others with you. You will find that success is much sweeter and more meaningful when it is shared with other people. Climb up, but reach down.

Don't wait for all the lights
to turn green; if you do, you'll
never leave your driveway.

JOHN C. MAXWELL

The world is round, so the place
which may seem like the end may
also be the beginning.

IVY BAKER PRIEST

*I*f you think you're
too small to have an impact,
try going to sleep with a
mosquito in the room.

ANITA RODDICK

Change something about your demeanor that will make other people feel more comfortable around you. This is not an easy charge to follow through on, but it is an important one. We would all like to think that we are seen only in a positive light by other people who know us, but that is almost never the case.

Have the courage to ask some people what you could do to help them feel more comfortable around you. Tell them to be completely honest...then allow yourself to become a better person by taking to heart what you're told.

*H*e who walks in another's
tracks leaves no footprints
of his own.

JOAN L. BRANNON

*W*hen you base your life
on principle, 99 percent of your
decisions are already made.

SOURCE UNKNOWN

*L*ots of people want
to ride with you in the limo,
but what you want is someone
who will take the bus with
you when the limo
breaks down.

OPRAH WINFREY

$\mathcal{D}$o something really special
for someone, but challenge yourself
to do it for a person who cannot pay you
back. More importantly, do it anony-
mously. One can never be considered
truly generous if something is done or
given with the expectation that something should come back to the one who
gave first. Always do and give for
the right reasons.

The best place to find a helping hand is at the end of your own arm.

SWEDISH PROVERB

Remember that the bread you meet each day is still rising. Don't scare the dough.

MACRINA WIEDERKEHR

If a small thing has
the power to make you angry,
does that not indicate
something about your size?

SYDNEY J. HARRIS

*T*ake thirty minutes or so to talk with an elderly person who is not a member of your family. Ask about his or her greatest experiences in life. Find out what makes them who they are, their likes and dislikes. Our culture used to have a profound respect for older persons, but that mindset seems to have faded away. Do your part to reverse that trend. Pay attention to the older people that you encounter. Learn from their incredible wisdom. An amazing amount happened before you were born—they'd love to tell you about some of it if you'd give them the chance.

Remove failure as an option
and your chances for success
become infinitely better.

JOAN LUNDEN

Always hold yourself to a
higher standard than anyone
else expects of you.

HENRY WARD BEECHER

Courage is not the towering
oak that sees storms come and go;
it is the fragile blossom that
opens in the snow.

ALICE MACKENZIE SWAIM

$\mathscr{S}$trive to find something good

in everything—in everything! Always

remember that the most beautiful roses

bloom at the the end of thorny stems.

Don't give up on anyone or anything

in life. Never leave before the

miracle happens.

The secret of getting ahead
is getting started.

SALLY BERGER

The happiness of your
life depends upon the quality
of your thoughts.

MARCUS AURELIUS

The most important thing in communication is to hear what isn't being said.

PETER DRUCKER

For one full week, smile more than usual. Make those smiles bigger and better than ever before. As you probably know, studies consistently show that people like to be around other people who smile a lot. Since smiles are often contagious, you'll likely also see more pearly whites than you've seen in a while. After consciously smiling more for one week, perhaps the practice will lead you to do it on a permanent basis.

*U*nderstand that what you don't do can be a very destructive force.

ELEANOR ROOSEVELT

*M*ost men pursue pleasure with such breathless haste that they hurry right past it.

SOREN KIERKEGAARD

Three failures denote uncommon strength. A weak person had not enough grit to fail thrice.

MINNA ANTRIM

*T*ry to develop a deeper trust and faith in God while relying less on your own abilities, strengths and finite knowledge. Letting go of control is never an easy thing to do, but it really is essential if you're going to become all that you were meant to be. As Oliver Wendell Holmes, Jr. so aptly put it, "The great act of faith is when a man decides that he is not God."

$\mathcal{E}$ndeavor to live so
that when you die, even the
undertaker will be sorry.

MARK TWAIN

$\mathcal{F}$ortune does not change a
person; it simply unmasks him.

SUZANNE NECKER

Happiness is something
that comes into our lives
through doors we don't even
remember leaving open.

ROSE WILDER LANE

Welcome a new resident to your street or neighborhood by bringing them a small present. The gift doesn't have to cost that much, and it can be as simple as a dozen donuts, a batch of cookies, or a few fresh flowers. The point is that whatever you give them, your thoughtfulness will make them feel "at home" on the block and will ease their feeling of

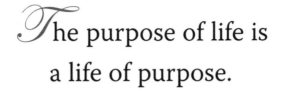

The purpose of life is
a life of purpose.

ROBERT BYRNE

Humility is like underwear—
essential, but indecent if it shows.

HELEN NEILSON

*B*eing powerful
is like being a lady. If you
have to tell people you
are, you aren't.

MARGARET THATCHER

*I*ncrease your use of the phrases "Please" and "Thank you." Be grateful for even the smallest things others do for you. National bestselling author Jeffrey Fox, in his famous book *How to Become CEO*, lists the top ten things you should say if you want to make someone feel good. According to his research, the most important thing you can say is "please"; in the number two spot is "thank you." Be polite and graceful at all times. Please, say "Thank you."

Silence at the proper
season is wisdom, and better
than any speech.

PLUTARCH

To be content with what
we possess is the greatest and
most secure of all riches.

CICERO

$\mathcal{B}$e a good example.
If you can't be a good example
then you'll just have to be
a horrible warning.

CATHERINE AIRD

Spend a day paying careful attention to those things around you that you normally take for granted. Find the beauty in details you usually over-look: the fine wood grain on a table, the movement of a candle's flame, a bee on a flower, the carbonation in a soda.... There is so much to miss in this world if we only look at the big picture.

You create your opportunities in life by asking for them.

PATTY HANSEN

To have and not to give is often worse than to steal.

MARIE VON EBNER-ESCHENBACH

*D*on't get to the end of
your life and find out that you
have lived just the length of it.
Live the width of it as well.

DIANE ACKERMAN

"*Raindrops* on roses and whiskers on kittens...." The song may be dated but the message most certainly isn't. Make a list of your ten favorite things in life, keep it in a convenient spot, and refer to it any time you're feeling down about something. You might be amazed at how much this can help!

My life is my message.

MAHATMA GANDHI

A minute's success pays
the failure of years.

ROBERT BROWNING

We would worry less
about what other people
think of us if we realized
how seldom they do.

ETHEL BARRETT

Whenever someone you know dies, write a brief letter to one of his or her survivors describing the impact—big or small—the person had on your life. If the person is too far removed from you to have had any impact at all, simply say something nice that you remember about the person or that you've heard about that individual. The recipient of the note will feel good reading it and you will likely feel good writing it; it will be 10 minutes of your time well spent.

A truth that's told with
bad intent beats all the lies
you can invent.

WILLIAM BLAKE

*N*o one can make
you feel inferior without
your consent.

ELEANOR ROOSEVELT

*A*ny concern too small to be turned into a prayer is too small to be made into a burden.

CORRIE TEN BOOM

$\mathcal{D}$o something to make a positive impact on a young child. Seemingly small acts from your viewpoint can often have a lasting, far-flung effect on a child. If nothing else, buy a couple boxes of cookies from a kid the next time he or she is selling them for a fund-raiser (never say "good luck" without purchasing their product!); consider giving them a small cash tip for their effort as well. The words that serve as the epitaph on Jackie Robinson's tombstone are worth noting here: "A life is not important except in the impact it has on other lives." Impact a child's life as soon as you can. Impact as many children's lives as you can.

*A*pplause is the spur
of noble minds, the end and
aim of weak ones.

CHARLES CALEB COLTON

*A*dmit your errors
before someone else
exaggerates them.

ANDREW V. MASON, MD

If we escape punishment
for our vices, why should we
complain if we are not
rewarded for our virtues?

JOHN CHURTON COLLINS

Call someone you haven't talked to in at least three years and rekindle an old friendship. If you're asking yourself why that person never calls you anymore, chances are they're wondering why you never call them! Put all your excuses away, take the initiative and dial them up. (Note: E-mailing them doesn't count. That's the easy way out, and the whole idea here is to experience a meaningful conversation with an old friend.)

*A*ll the sugar was in the
bottom of the cup.

JULIA WARD HOWE

*C*hoose a job you love
and you will never have to
work a day in your life.

CONFUCIUS

There is nothing wrong with making a silly mistake. Just be sure that you don't respond with an encore.

SOURCE UNKNOWN

*A*void snapping back the next time you're in a conversation and someone states an opinion that differs radically from your own. Don't even give the other person the chance to engage you in an argument (sometimes, that's all they're hoping to do by saying something they know bothers you). If you don't answer back, the discussion will quickly shift to another topic that more than likely won't ruffle your feathers. In life, pick all your arguments carefully; you'll rarely—if ever—win someone to your side by arguing with them, and being defensive just wastes a lot of time and energy that could be put to a lot better use.

People fail forward to success.

MARY KAY ASH

The direction of your
mind is more important
than its progress.

JOSEPH JOUBERT

Silence is the voice of the convinced. Loudness is the voice of those who want to convince themselves.

DAGOBERT RUNES

Celebrate a "Slow Down Week." That's right—a "Slow Down Week." Do everything at a decelerated pace from what you are used to—drive slower, walk slower, eat slower, speak slower, think slower...SLOWER is the word to remember. See if you can maintain this mindset beyond one week. And always keep this thought in mind: On life's highway, spend more time in the right-hand lane!

The whole is the sum
of the parts, so be a good part.

NATE MCCONNELL

You cannot do a kindness
too soon, for you never know
how soon it will be too late.

RALPH WALDO EMERSON

*S*triving for excellence motivates you, but striving for perfection will demoralize you.

DR. HARRIET BRAIKER

$\mathscr{B}$uy something for yourself that you really can't afford but that you also can no longer afford to go without. In other words, make a purchase that will make your life easier, more productive, or less stressful—thus paying significant "dividends" in the long run.

Talent is formed in stillness; character is formed in the world's torrent.

CHARLES JAMES FOX

Real happiness is cheap enough, but how dearly we pay for its counterfeit.

HOSEA BALLOU

When life knocks
you to your knees, get up!
If it knocks you to your knees
again—and it will—isn't
that the best position from
which to pray?

ETHEL BARRYMORE

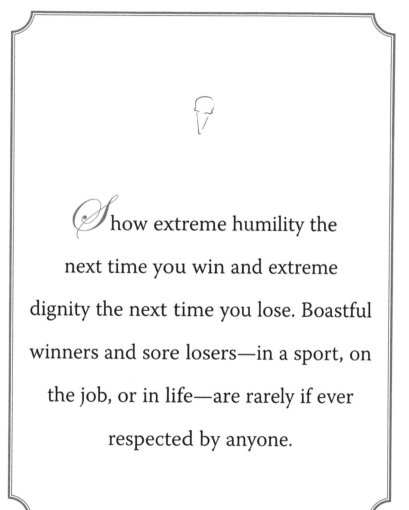

Show extreme humility the next time you win and extreme dignity the next time you lose. Boastful winners and sore losers—in a sport, on the job, or in life—are rarely if ever respected by anyone.

Nothing will ever content him who is not content with a little.

GREEK PROVERB

How exciting are your dreams? Most people don't aim too high and miss, they aim too low and hit!

BOB MOAWAD

*F*our steps to achievement:
plan purposefully, prepare
prayerfully, proceed positively,
pursue persistently.

WILLIAM A. WARD

Looking back at the past strains the neck muscles and causes you to bump into people not going your way.

EDNA FERBER

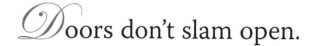

Doors don't slam open.

JOHN SHANAHAN

*Speak when you are
angry and you will make the best
speech you will ever regret.*

AMBROSE BIERCE

$\mathcal{D}$o not let what you
cannot do interfere with
what you can do.

JOHN WOODEN

$\mathcal{S}$ervice to others is the rent
we must pay for the privilege of
living on this earth.

SHIRLEY CHISHOLM

*G*od created the world
out of nothing, and as long as
we are nothing, He can make
something out of us.

MARTIN LUTHER

*F*ind a hero for yourself. We all need someone to inspire and motivate us to a higher level. Bernard Malamud, in *The Natural*, says it well: "Without heroes, we are all plain people and don't know how far we can go." The goal, of course, is not to be just like the hero; rather, simply let them inspire you to become better in your own unique talent or go farther in pursuit of your own special dreams.

*I*f you can learn from hard knocks you can also learn from soft touches.

CAROLYN KENMORE

A long life may not be good enough, but a good life is long enough.

BENJAMIN FRANKLIN

A man ninety
years old was asked to
what he attributed his
longevity. He responded,
"I reckon it's because most
nights I went to bed and slept
when I should have sat
up and worried."

DOROTHEA KENT

$\mathcal{L}$ie down in a field or park on a lazy summer day and spend some time simply watching the clouds roll by. Sit on a quiet shore and watch the summer sun set slowly over the water. Get away from the city lights and see the stars as they appear out in the country. Do all three of these things; as you do each one, consider how small your problems really are as you ponder the expanse of the universe.

*A*im at nothing and you'll
surely succeed.

SOURCE UNKNOWN

*O*ne who wants to
know is better than one who
already knows.

YIDDISH PROVERB

There are two kinds of people
on earth today, just two kinds of
people, no more, I say. Not the good
and the bad, for 'tis well understood
that the good are half-bad and the bad
are half-good. No, the two kinds of
people on earth I mean are the people
who lift and the people who lean.

ELLA WHEELER WILCOX

*H*appiness makes up in height
for what it lacks in length.

ROBERT FROST

*M*ost people spend more
time and energy going around
problems than trying to
solve them.

HENRY FORD

73

*N*ew things cannot come
where there is no room.

MARLO MORGAN

*O*ne person with passion
is better than forty who are
merely interested.

TOM CONNELLAN

It is right to be contented
with what you have, never
with who you are.

MACKINTOSH

I long to accomplish a great
and noble task, but it is my chief
duty to accomplish small tasks as
if they were great and noble.

HELEN KELLER

Everyone has an invisible sign hanging from their neck saying, "Make me feel important!" Never, ever forget this message when working with people.

MARY KAY ASH

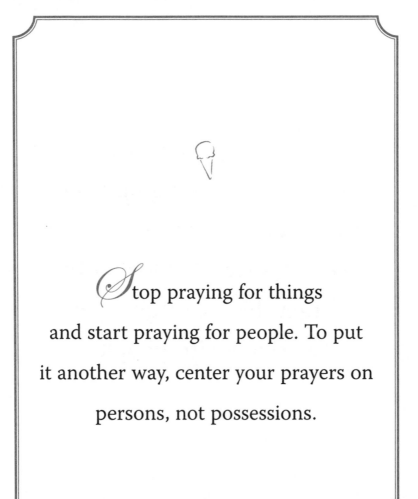

$\mathscr{S}$top praying for things
and start praying for people. To put
it another way, center your prayers on
persons, not possessions.

*W*orry is just like a rocking chair—it keeps you moving but doesn't get you anywhere.

CORRIE TEN BOOM

*I*t's not so much how busy you are that's important, but why you are busy. The bee is praised while the mosquito is swatted.

MARY O'CONNOR

*N*ever put off until tomorrow what you can do today, because if you enjoy it today, you can do it again tomorrow.

SOURCE UNKNOWN

Say "I love you" to someone who has rarely, or never, heard you say those words. It may not be the easiest thing you've ever done, but it just might end up being the best thing you've ever done.

$\mathcal{S}$ilence is golden,
so make your words platinum.

BRET NICHOLAUS

$\mathcal{A}$t least half the
troubles in life can be traced to
saying yes too quickly and not
saying no soon enough.

JOSH BILLINGS

A certain amount of opposition is a great help to a person. Kites rise against, not with the wind.

JOHN NEAL

A positive attitude may not solve all your problems, but it will annoy enough people to make it well worth the effort.

HERM ALBRIGHT

Some of the biggest failures
I ever had were successes.

PEARL S. BUCK

No one has a right to sit
down and feel hopeless. There's
too much work to do out there!

DOROTHY DAY

*T*act is the knack of making a
point without making an enemy.

SIR ISAAC NEWTON

*B*eing defeated is often only a
temporary condition. Giving up is
what makes it permanent.

MARLENE VOS SAVANT

When everyone is against you it means one of two things: Either you are absolutely wrong or you are absolutely right.

ALBERT GUINON

The next time you receive exceptional service in a mediocre restaurant, leave a 30 percent tip. It's only 15 percent more than customary, but it will mean a lot more than that to your server. On a $15 bill, an extra 15% is only $2.25 more than you'd normally tip; even on a $40 family-sized bill, you'd only be spending $6 more than usual. Since exceptional service really is a rare thing these days, it should be recognized and encouraged by rewarding it.

*C*ourage is fear holding on
a minute longer.

GEORGE S. PATTON

*T*he art of being happy lies in
the power of extracting happiness
from common things.

ARNOLD H. GLASOW

When you get into a
tight place and everything
goes against you, when it seems
as though you could not hang on
a minute longer, never give up
then—for that is just the place
and time that the tide
will turn.

HARRIET BEECHER STOWE

$\mathcal{S}$it down and write five jokes about yourself. If you don't feel like writing out the jokes, simply lie down on the couch and make fun of yourself for ten minutes or so. This may sound utterly ridiculous, but, all kidding aside, there is a real benefit that comes from doing this. By learning to take yourself lightly, you won't get so defensive when other people allude to your flaws and foibles. So go ahead: Have a good laugh at yourself!

Make no little plans; they have
no magic to stir men's blood.

DANIEL BURNHAM

Character is doing what's
right when nobody's looking.

J.C. WATTS

Negative thinking
can blind you to the good
that is out there, but you will
never ruin your eyesight
by looking on the bright
side of things.

SOURCE UNKNOWN

*O*ur greatest weakness lies in giving up. The most certain way to succeed is always to try one more time.

THOMAS EDISON

I make myself rich
by making my wants few.

HENRY DAVID THOREAU

*H*im for the top; there's plenty
of room there. There are so few at
the top, it's almost lonely.

SAMUEL INSULL

*I*f there is no wind,
you have to row.

LATIN PROVERB

*W*hether you think
you can or you think you
can't, you're right.

HENRY FORD

*S*ainthood emerges when you can listen to someone else's tale of woe without responding with a description of your own.

DR. ANDREW V. MASON, MD

$\mathcal{O}$ffer a piece of potentially
life-changing advice to someone you
know and care about. Offer it with
extreme tact and gentleness;
don't force it on the person.

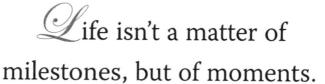

*L*ife isn't a matter of
milestones, but of moments.

ROSE KENNEDY

*W*on't you come into
my garden? I would like my
roses to see you.

RICHARD BRINSLEY SHERIDAN

Happiness consists of living each day as if it were the first day of your honeymoon and the last day of your family vacation.

SOURCE UNKNOWN

$\mathcal{G}$o an entire day without saying
one negative comment about anyone.
As soon as you catch yourself saying
even the slightest thing bad about someone, you must start over on another day.
To really test your resolve on this one,
pick a day when there will be plenty
of opportunities for you to talk about
other people—at a party, for example.
Can you extend your positive talk
beyond one day? Beyond two?
How far can you take it?

The less you talk,
the more you're listened to.

ABIGAIL VAN BUREN

One cannot possibly
collect all the beautiful shells
on the beach. One can collect
only a few, and they are more
beautiful if they are few.

ANNE MORROW LINDBERGH

I am truly convinced that
there are times in everybody's
life when there is so much to be
done that the only way to
do it is to sit down and
do nothing at all.

FANNY FERN

$\mathcal{D}$o like Duke! Jazz-great Duke Ellington was once asked what motivated him to write so many incredible tunes. Duke replied, "I merely took the energy it takes to pout and wrote some blues." The next time you're feeling bad, upset, bitter, or frustrated, take your negative energy and immediately use it to do something positive—something that will make you feel better physically, mentally and/or spiritually. If nothing else, your activity can be as simple as picking up the phone and calling someone you know who's a highly positive person and can help to cheer you up.

*T*he best thing about
the future is that it comes only
one day at a time.

ABRAHAM LINCOLN

*P*eace is not the absence of
conflict, but the presence of God
no matter what the conflict.

SOURCE UNKNOWN

We can learn much
from a kitten. It is chiefly
remarkable for rushing about
like mad at nothing whatever,
and generally stopping
before it gets there.

AGNES REPPLIER

$\mathcal{W}$rite yourself an IOU that comes due in six months and put it in an envelope. Write down whatever it is that you feel you owe yourself. A vacation? A new TV? A healthier body? A different job? Understand that you now owe it to yourself to accomplish or fulfill whatever you've written on that piece of paper.

Do not default!

In prosperity our
friends know us; in adversity
we know our friends.

JOHN CHURTIN COLLINS

Pleasure is very seldom
found where it is sought. Our
brightest blazes are commonly
kindled by unexpected sparks.

SAMUEL JOHNSON

*I*t is one of the most
beautiful compensations
of this life that no man can
sincerely try to help another
without helping himself.

RALPH WALDO EMERSON

$\mathcal{C}$ommit to memory at least one inspiring quotation per week. In one year, you'll know more than 50 bits of wisdom that you can instantly call upon whenever the need arises. After memorizing the quote, be sure that you actually do your best to follow the advice that each quotation offers—which is of course the point of memorizing the quote in the first place. (Unfortunately, what Yula Moses once said is true: Wisdom is much harder to do than it is to know.)

Sleep, riches and health
to be truly enjoyed must
be interrupted.

JOHANN PAUL FRIEDRICH RICHTER

Wherever we look on
this earth, the opportunities take
shape within the problems.

NELSON ROCKEFELLER

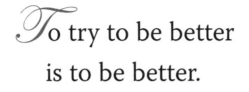

To try to be better
is to be better.

CHARLOTTE CUSHMAN

If you want to know how
rich you really are, find out what
would be left of you tomorrow
if you should lose every
dollar you own tonight.

W.J. BOETCKER

$\mathcal{R}$e-read a favorite book from your childhood. Get into it, enjoy it, allow yourself to be a kid again. Be careful that you don't overlook the moral of the story; it is probably as applicable to you as an adult as when you were a child.

*H*elp others get ahead. You always stand taller with someone else on your shoulders.

BOB MOAWAD

*I*t is a good thing to take long pauses in our pursuit of happiness and just be happy.

SOURCE UNKNOWN

Do not worry; eat three square meals a day; say your prayers; be courteous to your creditors; keep your digestion good; exercise; and go slow and easy. Maybe there are other things your special case requires to make you happy, but, my friend, these I reckon will give you a real good lift.

ABRAHAM LINCOLN

When because of your
worries you can't go to sleep,
just talk to the Shepherd and
stop counting sheep.

SOURCE UNKNOWN

*T*he world always steps
aside for people who know
where they're going.

MIRIAM VIOLA LARSON

*B*lessed is the person
who, having nothing to say,
abstains from giving wordy
evidence of the fact.

GEORGE ELIOT

$\mathcal{B}$e a lighthouse, not an outhouse! It's time to be really honest with yourself for a moment: Does the message your life sends to the world shine—or does it stink? Are you making the world a better place or are you making it a bitter place? Again, be completely honest with yourself as you think about this. If you truly believe that your light *does* shine in the world, how much brighter could your beacon be? A little brighter? Perhaps a lot brighter? Every day, in every way, live a life that is full of light, hope, joy, and love. In short, be a lighthouse, not an outhouse!

My advice to you is not
to inquire why or whither, but
just enjoy your ice cream
while it's on your plate.

THORNTON WILDER

About the Authors

Bret Nicholaus and Paul Lowrie are the authors of 17 books, including the national bestsellers *The Conversation Piece* and *The Christmas Conversation Piece*; other popular titles include *KidChat*, *The Christmas Letters*, *Lemonade Lessons for Life*, and *Who We Are*. The goal of all their books is to provide the reader with content that is highly positive and uplifting. Nicholaus and his family live in the Chicago area; Lowrie lives in South Dakota. If you would like to learn more about the authors or their books, you can do so by connecting to their website, www.williamrandallpublishing.com.

PHILIPPIANS 4:8-9

William Randall Publishing

publishes books that inspire people
of all ages to imagine the impossible,
to discover the profound in the ordinary,
and to keep life always in its proper perspective.

Our books are available in bookstores
everywhere. For a free catalog of our
complete line of fine books, contact:

William Randall Publishing
P.O. Box 340
Yankton, SD 57078

Phone: (605) 660-0335
Fax: (605) 260-6873

Email: questmarc@mail.com
Website: www.williamrandallpublishing.com